Published by Innovo Publishing, LLC
www.innovopublishing.com
1-888-546-2111

innovo
PUBLISHING

Providing Full-Service Publishing Services for Christian Authors, Artists & Ministries:
Books, eBooks, Audiobooks, Music, Screenplays, Film & Curricula

THE MERRY CHRISTMAS TREE FARM

Scripture is taken from the Holy Bible, New International Version®, NIV® Copyright ©1973, 1978, 1984, 2011 by Biblica, Inc.® Used by permission. All rights reserved worldwide.

ISBN: 978-1-61314-897-6

Cover Design & Interior Layout: Innovo Publishing, LLC

Printed in the United States of America
U.S. Printing History
First Edition: 2022

Has God called you to create a Christian book, eBook, audiobook, music album, screenplay, film, or curricula? If so, visit the ChristianPublishingPortal.com to learn how to accomplish your calling with excellence. Learn to do everything yourself, or hire trusted Christian Experts from our Marketplace to help.

christian
PUBLISHING PORTAL

THE MERRY CHRISTMAS TREE FARM

SHARON M. HAWKINS

innovo PUBLISHING

Hayden and his family were on their way to the Christmas Tree Farm. They were going to choose and cut their favorite Christmas tree. Hayden invited his friend Gabby to come along for their annual trip. Hayden and Gabby were so excited! Their hearts were thumping like the beat of the little drummer boy. *Pa-rum pum pum pum.*

During their car ride, Hayden told Gabby the story of how it all got started. He said, "The owners are Mr. Mullins and Ms. Norma. Mr. Mullins told me that they were planning for retirement and needed a side job. He said they were raising cattle, but the cows were always wandering off the property and getting into mischief.

"So, they had to come up with a new plan. They decided to plant Christmas trees on their 40-acres of land. Mr. Mullins said the only way a Christmas Tree would leave the property was if it was tied onto the roof of a vehicle."

Gabby chuckled and said, "That's a funny way to start a Christmas tree farm, but I'm sure glad they did."

Hayden proclaimed, "There it is! Right at the top of the hill. There's the Merry Christmas Tree Farm."

Gabby said, "Aww, look at the cute little cabin with the red roof."

Hayden replied, "The gift shop is always decorated in a different theme every year. I've heard that the family calls it *The Sugar Shack*."

Gabby was puzzled. She wrinkled up her nose and asked, "The Sugar Shack? Why do they call it that?"

Hayden said, "Well, Mr. Mullins built it with his own hands for his wife, Ms. Norma."

Gabby smiled and said, "Now that is about as sweet as some sugar. Haha, see how I just did that? Sweet? Sugar?"

Hayden rolled his eyes and said, "Yeah, haha, if you say so."

Gabby replied, "Shu-ga, shu-ga."

Their adventures were about to begin. Hayden's dad pulled into the driveway and parked the car. Hayden and Gabby hopped out of the car with jubilation. Gabby exclaimed, "Mmm, what's that smell? It smells like apples and maybe cinnamon?"

Hayden said, "I bet that is the hot apple cider that Ms. Norma always makes."

Gabby said, "Come on, let's go taste it!"

As they approached the gift shop, they saw Ms. Norma. She was whistling while sweeping the porch. Hayden told Gabby, "She always has a lot of gitty up in her step." They walked up the stairs, and Ms. Norma turned to greet them. Her whole face lit up. She was beaming from ear to ear. Her blue eyes were shining like diamonds. She stretched her arms out to welcome them to the farm.

Hayden hugged Ms. Norma and introduced Gabby. Ms. Norma smiled at Gabby and said, "It's so nice to meet you. I just made some hot apple cider. Follow me for a tasty treat!" Ms. Norma poured them some cups of hot apple cider. You could see the steam rising up out of the cups.

They started drinking, and Gabby said, "Yum-my, this is delicious! It tastes like warm apple pie."

Fresh Christmas Cut Trees

HOT

APPLE CIDER

All of a sudden they heard a bold, deep voice that said, "HO HO HO! MERRY CHRISTMAS."

Gabby was startled and asked, "What was that?"

Hayden grinned and said, "Look, it's that Santa over there in the corner. Let's check him out. He not only talks . . . he sings and dances."

Santa started singing, "We wish you a Merry Christmas, we wish you a Merry Christmas."

Hayden and Gabby started singing with Santa, "We wish you a Merry Christmas and a Happy New Year." They danced with Santa for a little while but then decided it was time to go on a hay ride.

As they walked toward the tractor, Gabby said, "Oh, that was fun."

Hayden said, "Yeah, but now the real fun starts. Let's climb on the hay ride with Mr. Mullins. We need to find the perfect Christmas tree." They stepped up onto the trailer that was hitched to the tractor. Gabby found them a seat on the hay beside Hayden's younger brother, AJ. There was another family on the ride that was all dressed in matching outfits.

The tractor started rolling, going toward the trail to the Christmas tree fields. Out of the blue, AJ shouted, "Quick, look, there's Wudolph!"

Mr. Mullins stopped the tractor and turned around. He said, "Yes, AJ, Wudolph the Reindeer checks out the tree farm. He makes sure that Santa has a clear runway to deliver toys in the neighborhood on Christmas Eve." AJ squealed and giggled. Everyone on the hay ride had a good chuckle too.

Hayden said, "On the way to the Christmas tree fields, we will cross over the bridge that Mr. Mullins built for Ms. Norma."

Perplexed, Gabby said, "What? So he built the Sugar Shack and the bridge for Ms. Norma?"

Hayden replied, "Yes, and he also carved Ms. Norma's name in the concrete floor of the bridge."

Gabby smiled and said, "Aww, he must think she is really special."

Hayden cleared his throat and said, "My mom says they have the sweetest love story."

Gabby replied, "Hubba, hubba."

The tractor started rolling through the bridge. Hayden said, "Look, here's where Mr. Mullins carved Ms. Norma's name!"

Gabby looked over the side of the trailer and said, "Wow, she's like a rock star in the hall of fame."

NORMA

"Speaking of rock stars, you didn't tell me that a grouch would be here," Gabby said.

Hayden chuckled and said, "You never know who might show up on the Christmas Tree Farm. It looks like a family invited a familiar green friend for their annual photo shoot."

The tractor soon came to a halt in a wonderland of Christmas trees. Hayden and Gabby jumped off the trailer. Hayden exclaimed, "Come on, let's play a game of hide-and-seek. I bet we will find the perfect Christmas tree." They ran in and out of the rows of trees. Everyone could hear the countdown: "10, 9, 8, 7, 6, 5, 4, 3, 2, 1. Ready or not, here I come!"

They played several games until they stumbled upon a tree that they both really liked. Hayden put his hand on the trunk and said, "This tree is really tall, thick, and wide. It also has strong branches to hold our ornaments."

Gabby replied, "Ahh, it smells so good too. This is the one!"

Mr. Mullins walked over with a big grin on his face. He asked them if they wanted him to cut it down. Hayden said, "Yes, this is the perfect Christmas tree."

Gabby said, "Quick, let's take a selfie with our tree before Mr. Mullins cuts it down!"

Mr. Mullins cut the tree down and loaded it into the trailer. Hayden and Gabby jumped onto the hay ride with their perfect Christmas tree. As they rode back from the fields, Hayden told Gabby, "When we get to the gift shop, they will place our tree into a shaker."

Gabby said, "Uh, what's a shaker?"

Hayden replied, "It shakes out any leaves, squirrels, and insects."

Gabby's eyes opened up really big. She responded in a high voice, "Squirrels?"

Hayden giggled and said, "Just kidding, but I suppose if there were any animals in there, they would shake out."

About that time, the tractor stopped. Mr. Mullins took the tree off the trailer and placed it into the shaker. The shaker was pretty loud and made the tree look like it was dancing. Gabby couldn't help herself. She started dancing and singing, "Shake, shake, shake . . . shake your booty, shake your booty."

Hayden looked at Gabby and said, "Really?" She stopped singing and dancing. She just shrugged her shoulder, looked at him, and smirked.

Then, all of a sudden, Hayden busted out a move and sang, "Shake your booty."

Gabby pulled out her phone and started her video app. She said, "Hayden, you're about to be famous!"

Hayden explained what happens next in the process. He said, "They will put our tree into the baler. It wraps the branches up tight with netting for easy handling."

Ms. Norma walked out of the gift shop and hopped down the stairs. She picked up one end of the tree to help Mr. Mullins guide it through the baler. Gabby said, "Wait a minute, where did Mr. Mullins go?"

Hayden chuckled and said, "He reached inside the baler to get our gigantic tree and pull it through. Kids, don't try this at home, haha! Whew, our tree made it through. Now they will carry it to our car and tie it on top of the roof for its journey home."

"Meanwhile, Mom will go into the Sugar Shack, I mean, the gift shop to pay for the Tree," Hayden said.

Gabby smiled and said, "Let's go inside so we can look at the ornaments."

Hayden replied, "Yes, let's go. We always get a new ornament here every year."

Gabby and Hayden walked into the gift shop. Christmas music was playing, and the air smelled like peppermint candy canes. Gabby's eyes opened really wide. You could hear her catch her breath. She said, "Ooh la la, my eyes are dancing. Helllloooo, gorgeous! I don't know where to look first!" There was glitter and sparkles, and there were lights, nativities, Santas, angels, handmade wreaths, gingerbread houses, and ornaments. Gabby started singing in an operatic voice, "Joy, joy, joy!"

Oh Holy Night

Joy to the World

Gingerbread St.

Ms. Norma hopped up with a big smile on her face and some gitty up in her step. She said, "Let me show y'all the new stuffed animals and toys we have."

Hayden picked up a stuffed monkey and put him around his shoulders. Gabby went straight to the nativity ornaments. She said, "Oh, I love this one with the baby Jesus."

Ms. Norma said, "Gabby, since this is your first visit to the tree farm, please accept this ornament as my gift to you."

Gabby smiled and said, "Oh, thank you so much, Ms. Norma. I can't wait to get the decorating party started at home. I will place this ornament on our Christmas tree first!"

Hayden's mom paid for the tree and the stuffed monkey. Ms. Norma smiled and said, "I hope to see you on the farm next year. Merry Christmas!"

Gabby and Hayden both said, "Merry Christmas!" at the same time. They looked at each other and said, "Jinx," and then started laughing.

Gabby and Hayden walked back to the car and jumped in. As the car drove out of the driveway, Gabby said, "Well, I'm sure going to tell my parents to come here next year."

Hayden smiled at her and said, "Oh, yeah, we're keeping the 'merry' in Christmas!"

One morning, eight years later, Ms. Norma was on the porch whistling while making apple cider. Mr. Mullins drove up on the tractor. Ms. Norma greeted him with some gitty up in her step and a cup of hot apple cider. She smiled and said, "Time to rise and shine."

Mr. Mullins grinned and said, "Yes, it is, pretty girl. It's gonna be a great day."

Meanwhile, a family drove into the farm for their first time. They were greeted by a vibrant set of teenagers. The young man said, "Hello, my name is Hayden." The young lady said, "Hi, my name is Gabby." Both teenagers said, "Welcome to Merry Christmas Tree Farm!" at the same time. They looked at each other and started laughing. The new family chuckled too. Hayden gave them the 411 on how to pick out the perfect Christmas tree. Then Gabby told them all about the Sugar Shack.

The real Mr. Mullins and Ms. Norma

For my precious mama, Ms. Norma; my bonus dad, Mr. Mullins; my brothers, John and Dewey; my husband, Corkey; my mother-in-law, Joyce; my children, Amanda and Scott; my son and daughter-in-law, Matt and Lexi; my grandchildren, Hayden, AJ, Gabby, Cooper, Ryder, Luke, Brooks, Bo, and Sunni; my soul sister, Laura; all of our extended family members, friends, employees, and loyal multi-generational patrons of the Merry Christmas Tree Farm. A legacy of faith, family, love, and service.

Arise, shine, for your light has come, and the glory of the LORD rises upon you. (Isaiah 60:1)